The Lord of Life

The "I Am" Sayings of Jesus

by
Merrill S. Williams

Beacon Hill Press of Kansas City
Kansas City, Missouri

Dedication

TO RUTH VAUGHN

—Who awakened in me
the first faint desire
to seriously express myself in words,
—Who told me
I had something significant to say
until I began to believe it myself, and
—Who taught me
how to begin learning
this arduous but rewarding craft of
writing.

Contents

1

I am the bread of life.

JOHN 6:35.

Food to Spare . . . Starving to Death

Because bread gives, nourishes, and sustains life, it has been called the "staff of life." Jesus used bread to symbolize man's basic needs. He instructed His disciples to pray, "Give us this day our daily bread" (Matt. 6:11, KJV).

Because bread was so highly valued in the ancient Near East, it was never cut, only broken. To these so dependent on earth's fertility, to cut bread—the symbol of life—was to cut life itself.

Each year thousands of people in different parts of the world suffer undernourishment and even starve to death from the lack of the physical bread of life.[1] This year alone, 450 million will endure the agony of malnutrition.[2] In 1974, during the last world food crisis, 100,000 people in the Sahel (southern Sahara region of Africa) alone starved to death.[3]

As tragic as that is, even more tragic is that many, many millions are slowly starving to death from spiritual malnutrition. The deepest needs of the human spirit are not physical. Man craves far more than the fading fare of earth; he seeks a deeper nourishment. Jesus knew that. That's why He advised, "Do not work for food that spoils, but for food that endures to eternal life" (John 6:27).

Many, thinking they have eaten life's satisfying portion, are left with only a bitter taste and an unfulfilled hunger. Leo Tolstoy wrote:

> I loved, I was loved, I had nice children, a fine estate, fame, health, physical and intellectual strength. . . . Suddenly my life was stopped. I no longer had any desires, I knew there was nothing left to desire. I had arrived at the abyss, and I saw that in front of me there was only death. I, a healthy, and happy man, knew that I could live no longer.

Clara Teare expresses the deep feelings of a multitude of contemporary men and women:

> *All my lifelong I had panted*
> *For a draught from some cool spring*
> *That I hoped would quench the burning*
> *Of the thirst I felt within.*

A.   The Giving of the Living Bread

Using an object lesson in which over 5,000 participated, Jesus dramatized His ability to nourish the human soul. The crowd, however, sought the bread of life for purely selfish, physical reasons. As the Samaritan woman sought water, they stood near One able to give life, but they sought only bread.

The crowd clamored for a sign and reminded Jesus that in the desert their forefathers were provided manna from heaven for them to eat. They believed that someone had hidden a jar of manna in the ark in the first Temple.

They claimed that when the Temple was destroyed, Jeremiah had hidden the manna and would produce it when the Messiah appeared.[4] "If you are the Messiah," the crowd challenged, "reproduce the manna-miracle of Moses."

Jesus, however, corrected their ideas: "It is not Moses who has given you the bread from heaven" (John 6:32). On another occasion John wrote, "And we have seen and testify that the Father has sent his Son to be the Savior of the world" (1 John 4:14).

Sir Harry Lauder tells the following story. Every family that had lost a son in the Second World War was entitled to place a lighted star in their window. As a man and his son walked down a street in New York, the lighted windows captured the small boy's attention.

Each time they passed a window, the boy would clap his hands and say, "Oh, look, Daddy! There's another house that has given a son to the war. Look! There's one that gave two sons. And there's a house with no star at all."

As they walked, they came to a break in the houses, and the evening star illuminated the night sky. "Oh, look, Daddy!" the boy exclaimed. "God must have given His Son—He has a star in His window, too."[5]

When the crowd asked for this bread, Jesus jolted their materialistic minds by declaring, "I am the bread of life" (John 6:35).

How people would like to enjoy the Bread of Life, but they will not identify with the Lord of life. They want the benefits of the Bread but not the cost of the Cross that comes with it.

We cannot separate what Christ gives from what He is. We cannot take His teaching or His gifts without also taking Him. Stephen Neill writes:

> We might have expected Him to say, "I give the bread of life," "I show you the way," "I tell you the truth;" but He does not. He cannot separate His message from Himself. . . . He is Himself the center of His own message and of the challenge that He brings.[6]

The Bread is the Son, and the Son came down from heaven. Did only the arbitrary tax decree of a Roman ruler place Joseph and Mary in Bethlehem, "House of Bread," where Mary bore the Christ? Or did a sovereign God supernaturally arrange for the Bread of Life to be born in that symbolic city?

Barley—which constitutes much of the bread in the ancient Near East—is the coarsest and least valuable form of bread. What a picture of Jesus! He "made himself nothing, taking the very nature of a servant" (Phil. 2:7). He was the Bread of Life who came to the world unadorned, unassuming, unapplauded.

The day Abraham Lincoln was born, a neighbor called to a friend from town and asked, "Any news down at the village, Ezra?"

"Well, Squire McLean's gone to Washington to see Madison sworn in, and old Spellman tells me this Bonaparte fellow has captured most of Spain. What's new out here, neighbor?"

"Nothing at all, nothing at all, except for a new baby down at Tom Lincoln's house. Nothing ever happens out here."[7]

The world was blind to a baby born in a stable. But when Mary gave birth to Jesus in Bethlehem, "the Word

was made flesh, and dwelt among us" (John 1:14, KJV).
Laurence Houseman put it like this:

> *Light looked down and beheld Darkness.*
> *"Thither will I go," said Light.*
> *Peace looked down and beheld War.*
> *"Thither will I go," said Peace.*
> *Love looked down and beheld Hatred.*
> *"Thither will I go," said Love.*
> *So came Light and shone.*
> *So came Peace and gave rest.*
> *So came Love and brought Life.*

The Son came down from heaven to *give up* His life. "He humbled himself and became obedient to death—even death on a cross!" (Phil. 2:8). Prophetically, the roads of Galilee led to Golgotha.

And when Jesus gave His life, He *gave us* life. John wrote, "The bread of God is he who comes down from heaven and gives life to the world" (John 6:33). "In him was life" (John 1:4), and in Him we live!

B.   The Eating of the Living Bread

Jesus is the Bread of Life. But we may still starve to death if we do not eat that life-giving and life-sustaining Bread.

How may a person partake of this spiritual nourishment?

1. *No one enters the banquet hall to dine whom the Father does not invite.* Jesus declared, "No one can come to me unless the Father who sent me draws him" (John 6:44).

The word "draw" John uses is the same word found in the Greek translation of Jeremiah. God speaks to the prophet, telling him, "Yea, I have loved thee with an everlasting love: therefore with lovingkindness have I drawn thee" (Jer. 31:3, KJV).

William Barclay says the word always implies some kind of resistance. Luke uses the word in Acts 16:19 to describe Paul and Silas being dragged before the magistrates in Philippi.

The human heart naturally—or should we say unnaturally—resists God's loving entreaty. We want to surrender, and we don't want to surrender. A battle rages within. God woos to win our allegiance; Satan fights to frustrate our allegiance. Paul graphically describes this mutiny of mind and heart in this way: "For what I want to do I do not do, but what I hate I do. . . . I have the desire to do what is good, but I cannot carry it out" (Rom. 7:15, 18).

2. *Some whom the Father invites eat.* John employs two metaphors in this passage to symbolize faith—coming and eating. Four times in this chapter Jesus speaks of men coming to Him (vv. 37, 44-45, 65).

Everyone who comes to Jesus in faith and commitment receives a satisfying portion. Jesus still extends the blessed invitation for all hungry souls. "Come unto me, all ye that labour and are heavy laden, and I will give you rest" (Matt. 11:28, KJV).

Clara Teare expresses the alternate despair and delight of many hungering seekers who become happy finders:

> *Feeding on the husks around me*
> *Till my strength was almost gone,*
> *Longed my soul for something better,*
> *Only still to hunger on.*
>
> *Hallelujah! I have found Him—*
> *Whom my soul so long has craved!*
> *Jesus satisfies my longings;*
> *Through His blood I now am saved.*

Eating the Bread of Life also symbolizes believing. Jesus said, "If a man eats of this bread, he will live forever. . . . Whoever eats my flesh and drinks my blood has eternal life" (John 6:51, 54).

These words do not refer to the sacrament of the Lord's Supper, but to the reality behind the sacrament. Those who hunger and thirst after righteousness shall be filled. They eat who appropriate or take for themselves possession of Christ's merits.

This word pierced to the heart of the casual acceptance of the crowd. It pointed inevitably to a crucial identification with Christ in death.

3. *Then, those who believe live.* Jesus said, "If a man eats of this bread, he will live forever. This bread is my flesh, which I will give for the life of the world" (v. 51). The life in the Bread is both present and future; it measures both its duration and its quality. Jesus said, "Now this is eternal life: that [men] may know . . . Jesus Christ, whom you have sent" (17:3).

When we eat the living Bread, Jesus imparts a new life that has no resemblance to evil; and therefore, we need not fear extinction. Death is only a minor jolt on the way from earth to heaven.

A woman I know lies dying of cancer in the hospital. They are no longer feeding her; she waits to die. But she has eaten of the Bread of Life; and when her body expires, she will not die but merely pass into a greater, fuller, more abundant life.

Lee Fisher asked his father if he had made plans for his and his wife's burial. His father said in astonishment:

> Son, I'm not making a date with the undertaker,
> I'm expecting the Overtaker. If I go to be with the Lord,
> you can put this body any place you like; but I'll not be
> in it. When you have a mansion in the sky, you can't
> become too excited about a lot in the cemetery.[8]

Are you pouring all your energy into making more money, accumulating more things, creating more hunger?

Isaiah asks a penetrating question: "Wherefore do ye spend money for that which is not bread? and your labour for that which satisfieth not?" (55:2, KJV).

Jesus offers a satisfying portion to the hungry-hearted men and women of earth, declaring, "I am the bread of life."

2

I am the light of the world.
JOHN 8:12

Light to Life

Jerusalem teemed with pilgrims who had come to celebrate the Feast of Tabernacles, one of three main religious holidays the Jews celebrated each year. For seven days the devout gathered to commemorate the wilderness wandering of their ancestors.

During 40 futile years God's people reaped a harvest of disobedience; and God led them, during the day by a cloud and during the night by a pillar of fire (Exod. 13:21-22).

Each night during the feast, the people enacted a special ceremony. As darkness descended on the Court of the Women, the priests lit four huge candelabra fitted with wicks made from the worn-out clothing of the priests. All night the people danced, and the Levites sang psalms.

The morning after the seventh day, Jesus stood near the Temple treasury and boldly proclaimed, "I am the light of the world" (John 8:12). He declared that He had fulfilled and replaced their festival. "You no longer need your elaborate candelabra," Jesus told them. "God is present in Me."

Different religions have explained good and evil in terms of light and darkness. The ancient Egyptians worshipped the brightest light they knew—the sun.

Light is also a familiar term in the Bible. Isaiah portrays the Messiah as a light. He wrote, "I will also give thee for a light to the Gentiles, that thou mayest be my salvation unto the end of the earth" (49:6, KJV).

On the first page of the Old Testament Moses describes God's creation of light (Gen. 1:3). On the last page of the New Testament John tells of heaven where "there shall be no night . . . and they need no candle, neither light of the sun; for the Lord God giveth them light" (Rev. 22:5, KJV).

Three stars of truth shine brightly in John's description of the Light of the World.

A. God's Presence

In Exodus God was present with His people in the pillars of cloud and fire. "And the Lord went before them by day in a pillar of a cloud, to lead them the way; and by night in a pillar of fire, to give them light; to go by day and night: he took not away the pillar of the cloud by day, nor the pillar of fire by night, from before the people" (13:21-22, KJV).

In the first century God was present among men in Christ. Christ's body, however, limited Him—He could only be one place at a time. But He promised that when He left, He would send another Comforter like himself to be with His people. "I will ask the Father, and he will give you another Counselor, to be with you forever—the Spirit of truth. . . . You know him, for he lives with you and will be in you" (John 14:16-17). With Frank Bottome we rejoice in His advent:

> *The long, long night is past;*
> *The morning breaks at last;*
> *And hushed the dreadful wail*
> *And fury of the blast,*
> *As o'er the golden hills*
> *The day advances fast!*
> *The Comforter has come!*

This Counselor, the Holy Spirit, is the Spirit of Christ (Rom. 8:9). Paul speaks of the possibility of God dwelling with us in the presence of Christ. He prays "that Christ may dwell in your hearts through faith" (Eph. 3:17).

Before John the Baptist appeared, the divine silence hung heavy over Israel for over 400 years. As in the days of Samuel, the glory had departed. In Christ, God restored the glory. "For in Christ all the fullness of the Deity lives in bodily form, and you have been given fullness in Christ" (Col. 2:9-10).

B. God's Guidance

God's specific guidance of His people is recorded in the ninth chapter of Numbers. The record leaves no doubt about who leads and who follows. God is in absolute command. When the cloud moved, the people marched. When the cloud stopped, the people camped. Whether the cloud of guidance tarried two days, or a month, or a year, the people waited until the Lord led.

Before Elijah's fiery ascent into heaven, God directed him from Gilgal to Bethel, from Bethel to Jericho, and from Jericho to Jordan. But God did not lead Elijah directly from Gilgal to Jordan. *He took him a step at a time.*

That's how God guides us—one step at a time. He discloses His will to us gradually. He does not give us a glimpse around every corner, or show us what lies beyond every crook in the road, or lay out a map which shows all the twists and turns that will eventually bring us into His presence. He knows that would overwhelm us, and He loves us too much to discourage us. He chooses to reveal only as much as we can presently accept.

A column of cloud and a pillar of fire forged a way for the Hebrews. We have a better guide in a world of greater complexities—the Spirit of Christ. Jesus promised, "When he, the Spirit of truth, comes, he will guide you into all truth" (John 16:13).

He is the guiding Light for Christians in the world!

C.   Man's Obedience

The sun may shine on the just and on the unjust alike. But the light of God illuminates only those who follow it. Jesus declared, "Whoever follows me will never walk in darkness, but will have the light of life" (John 8:12).

Jesus spoke these words on the morning when the celebrants would be making their journey from the holy city back to their homes, their businesses, and their daily responsibilities. He was saying to them, "You need not walk any longer in the darkness of your sin, and your fear, and your failure. You may forever live in the Light of Life."

Jesus reminded His disciples that "a man who walks by . . . night . . . stumbles, for he has no light" (John 11:9-10). But God "has rescued us from the dominion of darkness and brought us into the kingdom of the Son he loves, in whom we have redemption, the forgiveness of sins" (Col. 1:13-14).

Like Saul who fell stricken before the awful light of God on the Damascus Road, "the people that walked in darkness have seen a great light: they that dwell in the land of the shadow of death, upon them hath the light shined" (Isa. 9:2, KJV).

John delicately joins light and life. In light there is life; in life there is light. John expressly proposes to bring men to the Light to receive life (John 3:16; 20:31).

Enoch followed God and found life. He did not walk behind God. He did not walk ahead of God. He walked *with* God (Gen. 5:24). Saul stepped out too far in front of God's leading. The prophet Samuel clearly instructed Saul to wait until he returned and he would then offer the sacrifice. But Saul grew impatient, thought that just this once it would be all right, and went ahead and offered the sacrifice (1 Sam. 13:8-14).

Joshua instructed the people who were behind the Levites carrying the ark to leave "a space between you and it, about two thousand cubits by measure" (Josh. 3:4, KJV). Later when the oxen carrying the symbolic presence of God stumbled, Uzzah reached out to steady it, and God destroyed him. He stepped too far ahead of God's leading (2 Sam. 6:6-7).

It is also possible to walk behind God. Jonah did. God told him to go to Nineveh and conduct a revival campaign. Jonah—afraid of the will of God—travelled swiftly in the opposite direction. God shined the light of truth before him, and he refused to walk in it. Only after much persuasion did Jonah get back in step with God.

Peter also walked behind God. Luke records, "Peter followed at a distance" (Luke 22:54). Unfortunately, Peter usually receives all the blame because he followed "afar off." But the other disciples were not even following afar off! Should we not praise Peter for at least following? But not until Peter fully surrendered his life to God and allowed the Holy Spirit to cleanse his heart, did he get in proper step with God and begin to follow closely.

Kenneth L. Wilson recalls landing at an airport and seeing a small pickup truck dash in front of the taxiing plane. As the truck swung around, the passengers could read a large yellow sign with black letters attached to the tailgate. It read, "Follow Me." Mr. Wilson writes, "The sign didn't say, LISTEN TO ME. It didn't say, I'LL TELL YOU WHERE TO GO. It said, FOLLOW ME. That means GO WHERE I GO; DO WHAT I DO. And our plane did just that, and presently we were pulling up to our gate."[1]

Our greatest motivation for obedience is the personal example of Jesus. If we follow Him, we will truly walk with God.

In order to follow Him, however, we must surrender to Him, we must be willing to follow where the Light leads. The same pillar of fire that *beckoned* the Israelites *blinded* the Egyptians. "And it [the pillar] came between the camp of the Egyptians and the camp of Israel; and it was a cloud and darkness to them, but it gave light by night to these" (Exod. 14:20, KJV).

An anonymous author penned these appropriate lines:

> *Light obeyed increaseth light,*
> *Light resisted bringeth night.*
> *Who shall give me will to choose*
> *If the love of light I lose!*
>
> *Haste, my soul, this instant yield.*
> *Let the light its sceptre wield.*
> *While thy God prolongs His grace,*
> *Haste thee to His loving face.*

Jesus said, "I am the light of the world." Let us walk in that Light.

3

I am the door . . . I am the good shepherd.

JOHN 10:9, 11, KJV

I Stand by the Door

Some misguided individuals identify goodness only by its moral correctness, its sternness, its austerity. While not its primary meaning, the original rightly allows for "good" to be translated "beautiful."

When Jesus called himself the Good Shepherd,[1] He intended to paint a living picture of the beauty of goodness. He wanted to show that goodness is also attractive. When God assured Jehoshaphat that the battle was God's and not his, the grateful king "appointed singers unto the Lord . . . that should praise the *beauty* of holiness" (2 Chron. 20:21, KJV).

In these verses John leads us to drink at three springs of truth.

A. Intimately Acquainted

Since sheep in the Near East serve primarily for their wool and not for their meat, they may remain with the shepherd for years. He comes to look upon them not as animals but as friends. Because they are his friends, he names them. Usually the names describe some physical characteristic about the sheep like "Brown-leg" or "Black-ear."[2]

Not only did the shepherd know his sheep, but the sheep knew their shepherd. The shepherds in the villages corralled their sheep in communal folds, and several flocks might stay in the same fold. The only way to separate the sheep was for the shepherd to call his own. Since the sheep knew the shepherd, they responded to his voice. They never went to the wrong shepherd.

Some have dressed in the shepherd's garb and called the sheep to follow them. But they do not follow, because an alien voice sounds in their sensitive ears. They do not answer to other calls; they answer only to the authentic shepherd.

The Christian's Shepherd speaks through His Holy Spirit. His true sheep recognize His voice. Practice tunes their ears to pick up the distinctive sound of the Good Shepherd's voice.

Paul warns us that Satan "masquerades as an angel of light" (2 Cor. 11:14). At times our adversary will also attempt to disguise his voice and lead us astray, away from the safety of our Shepherd's fold. If we tune our ears and turn our hearts toward the Spirit, we can easily detect the false shepherd. An imposter cannot deceive us.

E. Stanley Jones tells how a sheepherder who lived alone on his ranch in Idaho discovered his violin was out of tune. But, in order to correct his problem, he needed a standard note. He wrote the radio station in California to which he listened and asked them to strike the note he needed.

On a certain day, they interrupted their regular programming and sounded the needed note. The rancher listened, caught the note, and put his violin back in tune.[3] When life tends to go flat, we need to ask God for His standard note to keep our lives tuned to His frequency.

When Elijah stood on the mountain, the Lord spoke to him not in the screaming wind, or the thundering earthquake, or the roaring fire; he whispered in "a sound of gentle stillness" (1 Kings 19:12, marg.). When the Spirit speaks to us, He will speak clearly, but gently. And when He speaks, we must listen carefully, quietly, reverently.

The Good Shepherd *leads* His sheep, He does not *drive* them. He "leads them out. . . . He goes on ahead of them" (John 10:3-4). Let us forever cast away the concept of a brutal, driving shepherd. Too often we fear a Lord who fails to even resemble the tyrant we envision. He leads with love. He does not drive with dread. G. A. Young expressed it this way:

In shady green pastures so rich and so sweet,
  God leads His dear children along.
Where the water's cool flow bathes the weary one's feet,
  God leads His dear children along.

When the Good Shepherd leads, the true sheep follows. "His sheep follow him because they know his voice" (v. 4). Phillip Keller, a modern-day shepherd, recalls an obstinate ewe on his ranch in South Africa. He called her "Mrs. Gad-about." She displayed a strong body, sported a fine coat of wool, and bore beautiful, healthy lambs. But her problem was her will.

Not content to stay in her own pasture, she continually searched for holes in the fence to sneak through and indulge in the neighbor's grass. Worst of all, however, she taught her lambs to follow her in disobedience. Rather than allow her to endanger the entire flock, Keller dispensed with her. She had refused to follow.[4]

B. Legitimately Attentive

Because "good" describes the character of our Shepherd, He consistently seeks the welfare of His sheep. He attends to their needs.

The word "shepherd" derives from a word that means "to protect." The shepherd spends a great deal of time protecting the flock and keeping them safe from the dangers that threaten them. Predators, parasites, hunger, and inter-flock rivalry all instill fear in the sheep.

Mr. Keller says that as few as two dogs have been known to slaughter as many as 292 sheep in one night.[5] The alert, attentive shepherd constantly watches for these perils to his flock. Matthew describes the Good Shepherd's concern for us: "When he saw the crowds, he had compassion on them, because they were harassed and helpless, like sheep without a shepherd" (9:36).

1. The Good Shepherd offers *safety*. He says, "Whoever enters through me will be saved" (John 10:9). The margin in the NIV reads "kept safe." In *God, Man, & Salvation* the authors write:

> The object of God's concern, man, comes immediately into view—with salvation, or redemption, as the purpose both of the covenant and the kingdom of God. *God and man in redemptive relationship is the theme of the Old Testament that extends into and throughout the New* [italics mine].[6]

But this salvation rests on an all-important condition—"Whoever enters." The door opens to all, the Good Shepherd provides salvation only to those who enter the fold through Him.

2. Our Shepherd offers not only safety but also *security*. "He will come in and go out" (John 10:9). The Hebrews used this phrase to describe a life free from danger. In terms of the sheep metaphor, it means that the sheep have a protected sphere in which to move.

Alexander Maclaren applies this phrase to the two sides of human activity—the inner life of spiritual contemplation and the outer life of practical obedience. Elton Trueblood called the interior life of devotion, the *roots* of Christian experience. He called the exterior life of service, the *fruits* of Christian experience.

Before we can go out to serve, we must come apart to pray. The disciples on the Mount of Transfiguration would have preferred to continue worshipping at the shrine of Christ's glorified presence. But a young epileptic boy waited below to receive the service they could render after having tarried with Jesus.

3. Not only does our Shepherd offer safety and security, but He also offers *sufficiency*. He says that "whoever enters through me will . . . find pasture" (John 10:9).

David, the shepherd-king, praises his Shepherd for preparing "a table before me in the presence of mine enemies" (Ps. 23:5). Phillip Keller says that the valuable pastureland in the highlands of some parts of the United States and southern Europe are called *mesas*. *Mesa* is the Spanish word for "table."

The "table" of the 23rd psalm is evidently the luscious summer range where the shepherd grazes his flock during the summer months. Here the sheep find an abundance of pasturage.[7]

Our Shepherd offers us an abundant measure of spiritual pasture. He promises, "I have come that they may have life, and have it to the full" (John 10:10). Barclay writes that the "phrase which is used for *having it more abundantly* [cf. KJV] is the Greek phrase which means to have *a surplus, a superabundance of a thing*. To be a follower of Jesus . . . is to have a superabundance of life."[8]

C. Ultimately Appointed

The shepherd was often called upon to defend his flock with his life. In 1 Sam. 17:34-37 David testifies before Saul that he often risked his life to guard his father's flock. The Good Shepherd will also be called upon to lay down His life for the sheep.

1. Jesus says that *He is an obedient shepherd*. "I lay down my life . . . No one takes it from me, but I lay it down of my own accord" (John 10:17-18). Paul said Jesus "humbled himself and became obedient to death" (Phil. 2:8).

Jesus surrendered His life voluntarily. When the soldiers arrested Jesus, one of His companions drew his sword and sliced off the ear of the high priest's servant. "Do you think I cannot call on my Father," Jesus asked, "and he will at once put at my disposal more than twelve legions of angels?" (Matt. 26:53).

In the First World War shrapnel so seriously injured a young French soldier that the surgeon amputated his arm. Because he was in the prime of youth, the surgeon waited for him to wake to inform him personally of his loss. When the boy opened his eyes, the surgeon said, "I am sorry to tell you that you have lost your arm."

"Sir, I did not lose it; I gave it—for France."[9]

No one took Jesus' life; He gave it—willingly.

Jesus' life-giving, however, differs dramatically from that of the typical Eastern shepherd. If the Palestinian shepherd died, he died by *accident*. But the Good Shepherd died by *appointment*. If the Palestinian shepherd lost his life, the sheep *suffered*. But when the Good Shepherd lost His life, the sheep *survived*.

2. Jesus also says *evangelism is an urgent task*. "I have other sheep that are not of this sheep pen. I must bring them also" (John 10:16). The word "must" epitomizes the urgency of the evangelistic task.

From the time Jesus uttered the words, "I must be about my Father's business" (Luke 2:49, KJV), until the day He cried, "Father, into your hands I commit my spirit" (Luke 23:46), Jesus poured himself into the task of bringing the lost sheep into the fold.

Jesus saw other sheep who belonged to Him, but who had not yet been brought into His fold. He sees many people in our spheres of influence who belong to Him. He is depending on you and me to harvest these potential disciples. May our hearts—preacher and layman alike—beat in time with Paul's evangelistic heart: "I am compelled to preach. Woe to me if I do not preach the gospel!" (1 Cor. 9:16).

Do we too often only see people as they *are*, when Christ wants us to see them as they might *become?* When Andrew brought his brother, Peter, to Jesus, the Savior looked at him and stated, " 'You are Simon, son of John' " (John 1:42). Peter's father had named him Simon. That name symbolizes Peter's character apart from Christ.

Jesus then went on to add, " 'You will be called Cephas' (which, when translated, is Peter)." His new name symbolized the vessel Jesus knew he could become in the Master Potter's hands.

It is told that someone came upon the great Michelangelo chipping away at a large piece of stone and asked him what he was doing. He answered, "I am releasing the angel imprisoned in this stone." God wants to enlist us to help Him release some potential angels.

Samuel Shoemaker wrote what he called "An Apologia for My Life" entitled "I Stand by the Door." He says:

> I stand by the door. . . .
> The door is the most important door in the
> world—
> It is the door through which men walk
> when they find God. . . .

The most tremendous thing in the world
Is for men to find that door—the door
to God.
The most important thing any man can do
Is to take hold of one of those blind,
groping hands,
And put it on the latch—the latch
that only clicks
And opens to the man's own touch.
Men die outside that door, as
starving beggars die
On cold nights in cruel cities in
the dead of winter—
Die for want of what is within their
grasp.
They live, on the other side of it—
live because they
have not found it.
Nothing else matters compared to
helping them find it,
And open it, and walk in, and find Him . . .
So I stand by the door. . . .

As for me, I shall take my old
accustomed place. . . .
Where? Outside the door—
Thousands of them, millions of them.
But—more important to me—
One of them, two of them, ten of them,
Whose hands I am intended to put on the
latch.
So I shall stand by the door and wait
For those who seek it. . . .
So I stand by the door.[10]

Let us also stand by the door to help the Good
Shepherd bring others to safety.

4

I am the resurrection and the life.
JOHN 11:25

The Lord of Life

Lazarus is dead. The awful thought drains slowly down through Martha's consciousness. Silently she asks in her mind the question that she, Mary, and the crowd would all ask later: "Where was Jesus? If He had been here, my brother would surely not have died."

But the story was not yet finished. A final chapter remained, and the Lord of Life would pen the lines. The name Lazarus means "God has helped." Even his name prophesied the victorious outcome of this sorrow-filled saga.

Lazarus' resurrection crowns the public ministry of Jesus leading up to the Cross and ultimately to His own resurrection. It is the last miracle John records before the Cross. Two others, however, preceded it. Jesus first raised the daughter of Jairus and the son of the widow of Nain.

The synagogue ruler's daughter may have been dead only a few minutes. Someone could argue she only *appeared* dead. The widow's son had died only hours before.

Anyone wishing to discount the miraculous element could argue he was only in a trance. But Lazarus had lain in the tomb four days. No one could possibly deny that when Lazarus came forth, he came forth *from the dead.*

Three lines of thought run through this chapter and tie together the meaning of Jesus' victory over death.

A. Life Depleted

The man named Lazarus and described as Mary's brother "now lay sick" (John 11:2) and would soon die.

1. What was *the purpose of the sickness?* Jesus explains that "this sickness will not end in death. No, it is for God's glory so that God's Son may be glorified through it" (v. 4).

Throughout His ministry Jesus consistently identifies His glory with His cross. "By this he meant the Spirit, whom those who believed in him were later to receive. Up to that time the Spirit had not been given, since Jesus had not yet been glorified" (7:39). In predicting His death, Jesus says, "The hour has come for the Son of Man to be glorified" (12:23). In His high-priestly prayer on the eve of His passion, Jesus prayed, "Father, the time has come. Glorify your Son, that your Son may glorify you" (17:1).

When Jesus said the sickness of Lazarus would glorify Him, He knew it meant His own death.

2. Then, there is *the peril of the Savior.* "Then he said to his disciples, 'Let us go back to Judea.' 'But Rabbi,' they said, 'a short while ago the Jews tried to stone you, and yet you are going back there?' " (11:7-8).

Some wonder why Jesus waited two days before going to Bethany. Many mistakenly think He waited for Lazarus to die in order to heighten the effect of the impending miracle. If Jesus waited two days before starting, and if we allow one day travel time each for the messengers and Jesus, then Lazarus probably died soon after the messengers left to find Jesus.

Why then did Jesus tarry? To emphasize that He acted only in conformity with His Father's will. Others had tried to influence Him. At a wedding in Cana His mother reminded Him the host had run short of wine. She expected Him to fill the jars. On another occasion His brothers tried to persuade Jesus to go to Judea and show off His miracle-making ability.

He did provide the wine, He did go to Judea (although secretly), and He did go to Bethany. But He went because He conceived it to be God's will.

Satan's subtle suggestions to Jesus in the desert involved doing God's will, but not in God's time and in God's way. Let us be certain we carefully perceive God's will and faithfully pursue it.

A lack of love did not keep Jesus from Bethany. John says, "Jesus loved Martha and her sister and Lazarus" (John 11:5). Because John lists them individually, we may assume Jesus loved them individually. He did not love the family. He loved Martha and Mary and Lazarus. When Jesus said, "For God so loved the world, that he gave his only begotten Son" (3:16, KJV), He said it to one man—Nicodemus.

To go to Bethany would cost Jesus His life. But He went because He loved Lazarus. He was just as determined to go to Jerusalem because He loved you and me. Luke says, "As the time approached for him to be taken up to heaven, Jesus resolutely set out for Jerusalem" (Luke 9:51). Jerusalem . . . Golgotha . . . a cross.

3. Next, Jesus describes *the posture of the sleeping*. "His disciples replied, 'Lord, if he sleeps, he will get better.' Jesus had been speaking of his death, but his disciples thought he meant natural sleep" (John 11:12-13).

New Testament writers frequently referred to death as sleep. But Jesus' disciples misunderstood. Jesus had to state plainly, "Lazarus is dead" (v. 14). Christianity contributed greatly to the ancient world's concept of death. While the ancients feared death, Christianity said Christ had removed the sting of death, sin (1 Cor. 15:56), and men need fear it no longer.

4. In the gloomy pronouncement of Thomas we glimpse *the promise of the surrendered.* "Then Thomas (called Didymus) said to the rest of the disciples, 'Let us also go, that we may die with him' " (John 11:16). In these words Thomas spoke more than he knew.

Thomas' declaration implies the symbolic death of the Christian by personal identification with Christ. Paul said, "Or don't you know that all of us who were baptized into Christ Jesus were baptized into his death? . . . In the same way, count yourselves dead to sin but alive to God in Christ Jesus" (Rom. 6:3, 11).

Grace Nies Fletcher grew up in a Methodist parsonage. When she was a teenager, her first love—who was the commanding officer at his military school—asked her to accompany him to the annual ball. Her parents, however, refused to let her go, and Bill took someone else.

In the days before the event she built a wall of bitterness in her heart toward her parents. On the night of the ball she lay upstairs in her room weeping. Through her sobs she detected her father's voice on the telephone.

"Hello, Henry? Henry, I've decided to sell my John Wesley *Journal.* I know how much you want a set. . . . Oh, you would? Fine. I'll deliver them tomorrow."

She heard her father phone again, and then he came up to her room. "Susie?" he said. "I've got a couple of tickets for the Boston Symphony. Will you go with me tonight?" Rather than lay and think about her beau with someone else, she reluctantly consented.

But as they entered the great hall and found their seats, she wondered how her father had been able to afford them. Suddenly she remembered the *Journal*. He had sold his beloved *Journal* to comfort her! She writes:

> As I looked up at his clear familiar bulk beside me, the bitterness seeped out of my heart. "You shouldn't have—" But my words were drowned out by the thunder of applause as Dr. Karl Muck strode out onto the stage . . . and mounted the podium to conduct the Fifth Symphony.
>
> He tapped his baton; there was a moment of silence and then the majestic music swept over us in a flood of glory. To me the music said . . . lose your smallness in My Greatness. . . . For the first time since I was born, I lost my little self in beauty bigger than I was.[1]

Jesus said, "The man who loves his life will lose it, while the man who hates his life in this world will keep it for eternal life" (John 12:25). If we would live in victory, the time must come in each of our lives when we die to Satan, to sin, and to self.

B.   Faith Completed

1. In the fourth "I Am" saying *Jesus confirms the fact of His conquest over death.* "I am the resurrection and the life" (11:25). He ties together resurrection and life. There is no resurrection without life; there is no life without resurrection. Jesus does not say He will give life, but that He *is* life.

This life is both a present reality and a future certainty. In the Christian, resurrection life reigns now. Jesus said, "Now this is eternal life: that they may know you, the only true God, and Jesus Christ, whom you have sent" (17:3). If we know Him, we *now* live in the realm of eternity.

If we know Him, the mist of the future clears. Death is only a momentary shadow that passes over life and ushers us into the presence of God. The eternal quality of resurrection life passes into infinite quantity.

E. Stanley Jones writes:

> Heaven and hell are not something God sovereignly gives you at the end of your earthly life. . . . If you take out heaven with you at the end of this life, you will get heaven, for you will have brought it with you—in you. . . . If you take hell out with you, you will get it, for you will have brought it with you—in you.[2]

2. When Jesus confirms the fact of His conquest over death, *Martha confesses her faith in the Christ of victory.* "I believe that you are the Christ, the Son of God, who was to come into the world" (John 11:27). John the Baptist testified about Jesus, "The one who comes from above is above all" (3:31).

C.   Death Defeated

When Jesus cried, "Lazarus, come out!" (11:43), He illustrated His earlier message, "I am the resurrection and the life" (v. 25). Lazarus' resurrection was a prelude to Jesus' resurrection and to our own.

In Nevil Shute's *A Town like Alice,* an Australian named Joe Harman helped a group of women prisoners being held by the Japanese in Malaya. The women suffered severely from undernourishment. Harman stole 5 of Captain Sugamo's 20 prize, black leghorn chickens and gave them to the women for food. When the captain discovered one-fourth of his imported-from-England chickens gone, he raged.

The soldiers questioned the group's spokeswoman, Jean Paget. She claimed Harman had given them money, and that they had bought the fowls. When the soldiers doubted her story, they slapped her in the face, kicked her in the shins, and stomped on her bare feet.

She tried not to implicate Harman. But when he saw her bleeding face and battered body, he said, "Leave her alone. . . . I stole those chickens and I gave them to her." The soldiers then took everybody back to town, nailed Joe Harman's hands to a tree, and apparently beat him to death—while the women watched.

Six years following the war, Jean Paget returned to the village to build a well for the poor villager women. She hired an old man, Suleiman, and his two sons, Yacob and Hussein, to dig the well. In conversation Jean mentioned that the wicked Captain Sugamo had been tried by the Allies for atrocities and executed. She also referred to the prisoner who had helped them and was crucified and beaten to death.

"Yes," said Suleiman. "He was in hospital in Kuantan."

"Old man, no, he died."

"Perhaps there were two." He called down the well to Yacob. "The English soldier who was crucified at Kuantan—tell us, did that man die?"

Hussein broke in. "The one who was crucified was an Australian, not English. It was for stealing the black chickens."

"But did he live or die?" the old man said.

Yacob called up from the bottom of the well. "Captain Sugamo had him taken down that night; they pulled the nails out of his hands. He lived."[3]

But Jesus died a real death, and He lives a truly resurrected life. We share in that life. Paul wrote, "To be sure, he was crucified in weakness, yet he lives by God's power. Likewise . . . by God's power we will live with him" (2 Cor. 13:4).

By this miracle in Bethany Jesus proved He is the Lord
of Life. And with Matthew Bridges and Godfrey Thring
we join to

> *Crown Him the Lord of Life!*
> *Who triumphed o'er the grave;*
> *Who rose victorious to the strife*
> *For those He came to save.*
> *His glories now we sing*
> *Who died and rose on high,*
> *Who died eternal life to bring,*
> *And lives that death may die.*

5

I am the way and the truth and the life.
JOHN 14:6

Up, Up, and Away

John Wesley wrote:

> I have thought, I am a creature of a day, passing through life as an arrow through the air. I am a spirit come from God, and returning to God: just hovering over the great gulf; till a few moments hence, I am no more seen; I drop into an unchangeable eternity! *I want to know one thing—the way to heaven"* [italics mine].

Multitudes join Mr. Wesley in his desire to "land safe on that happy shore." They seek the way to Life, to the Father, to heaven.

Three questions about heaven clamor to be answered.

A.   Heaven—Why Do We Want to Go There?

1. *The circumstances surrounding Jesus' fifth "I Am" saying spoke of trouble.*

   a. First, Jesus predicted His own *betrayal.* Jesus told His disciples, "One of you is going to betray me"

(John 13:21). The words fell on their ears like heavy stones. What did He mean? How could it be?

       b. Second, Jesus predicted His imminent *withdrawal.* "My children," He said, "I will be with you only a little longer" (v. 33). Again their confidence careened out of control. "How can He leave us after we have left all to follow Him?" they must have asked each other.

To make matters worse, Jesus told them they could not follow. Alexander Maclaren summarizes their fear: "They fancied that if He left them they lost Him."

       c. But Jesus will shoot another arrow into their already bleeding hearts—Peter's *denial.* Not only would a trusted disciple betray his Master. Not only would their beloved Lord leave behind His fearful disciples, but also the impetuous spokesman of the Jesus-band would deny his Lord. And not once, but three times!

What more could Jesus say to deflate their faith?

2. But immediately He comforts them. While the circumstances spoke of trouble, *the Savior spoke of trust.* "Do not let your hearts be troubled. Trust in God, trust also in me" (John 14:1). The original language inverts the second phrase, and the sentence reads, "Trust in God; in Me also trust." This places the divine Pair at the center, as close together as possible, fenced on all sides with faith.

We do not just blindly trust something; we trust Someone. That Someone reigns at the center of life; and, from the beginning of Christian experience to the end, we surround that center with trust.

We can trust Him because He gave all that was possible for Him to give. "He . . . did not spare his own Son, but gave him up for us all—how will he not also, along with him, graciously give us all things?" (Rom. 8:32).

Sometimes our personal world threatens to explode into a thousand tiny pieces. And although His presence sustains in the dark hours of sorrow, we look longingly for "a land that is fairer than day."

B.   Heaven—What Will We Find There?

Heaven is the heart of Jesus' comfort to His sagging disciples. He told them, "I am going there to prepare a place for you" (John 14:2). In Jesus' day it was customary to send an envoy ahead to prepare the way for others to follow. That very day Jesus had sent Peter and John into Jerusalem to make arrangements for the disciples to eat the Passover together (Mark 14:12-16).

The New Testament portrays Jesus as our Forerunner. The *Daily Study Bible Series* sheds meaningful light on the word. The harbor at Alexandria, Egypt, was so dangerous to approach that the harbormaster deployed a small pilot boat to guide the great corn ships safely into port.[1] This is the word used to describe Jesus. Our Forerunner "went before us" (Heb. 6:20) to prepare the way to heaven.

But He also promised to return for us. He said, "And if I go and prepare a place for you, I will come back and take you to be with me that you also may be where I am" (John 14:3).

Jesus never intended the truth of His second coming to be used to manipulate people. W. E. McCumber writes: "Sermons I have heard rarely sounded the note of encouragement. Instead, they were, to discerning listeners, an obvious attempt to bolster sagging attendance and a scare tactic to increase response."[2] Jesus intended these to be words of comfort.

1. Let us, therefore, take courage because *we will be at home in heaven.* Heaven will consist of many rooms. "Mansions"—the word we are familiar with—means "permanent residence." Many of us live in temporary housing, especially with the rising cost of buying a home.

But even homeowners reside only temporarily on earth. In heaven, however, everyone will own his own home!

A rabbinic tradition said that no matter how many thronged to Jerusalem for the Passover, the streets were never crowded. While we may doubt the truth of that tradition, we may be sure it is true of the New Jerusalem.

The home metaphor illustrates that we can have "a little heaven to go to heaven in"; that heaven is more than a place; that heaven is primarily a state of mind.

Later in this same chapter Jesus says, "If anyone loves me, he will obey my teaching. My Father will love him, and we will come to him and *make our home with him*" (John 14:23).

In the presence of the Holy Spirit, Jesus makes His home in our hearts. Paul says we are "marked . . . with a seal, the promised Holy Spirit, who is a deposit guaranteeing our inheritance until the redemption of those who are God's possession" (Eph. 1:13-14). By living in the Spirit, we now enjoy God's first installment of what heaven will be.

In E. Stanley Jones's last book, *The Divine Yes*, soon before he himself went to heaven, he wrote:

> Never have I emphasized "being in heaven" very much in my life, for I think I have had heaven here. . . . Finding Jesus as Savior and Lord and the Kingdom of God as the ultimate goal of the world and humanity has been sufficient to keep my faith in a world called heaven.[3]

2. Let us also take courage because *we will be with Jesus in heaven.* Paul said that to be away from the body is to be "at home with the Lord" (2 Cor. 5:8). Heaven would not be heaven without Him.

In an evangelistic service Evangeline Booth said:

> I want to see John Howard when the last prisoner shall have been reformed, and Florence Nightingale when the last wound shall have been staunched, and

John Hus when the last martyr fire shall have burned out, and William Penn when the last heathen shall have been civilized, and Frances Willard when the last lost girl shall have been won, and your great President Lincoln when the last slave shall have been made free, and my father and my mother; but most of all I want, and I want all of you, to see Jesus.

After serving in the Civil War, Sanford Bennett returned home to Elkhorn, Wis., to practice medicine. One day a friend, Joseph Webster, stopped to visit. But instead of chatting pleasantly as he usually did, Mr. Webster sat by the stove, withdrawn and quiet. He was obviously troubled.

Before long, however, he looked up and said, "It'll be all right by and by."

The words struck Bennett so forcefully that he sat down, took pen in hand, and began to write:

> There's a land that is fairer than day,
>   And by faith we can see it afar;
> For the Father waits over the way,
>   To prepare us a dwelling place there.

When clouds of trouble darken our skies, we can keep confident, knowing "it'll be all right by and by."

C.   Heaven—Who Will Take Us There?

Heaven, then, is our destination. But how shall we get there?

Jesus' disciples journeyed in a tunnel of spiritual darkness. They knew neither their destination nor the way to get there. In a sentence teeming with truth, Jesus shines an illuminating light on an otherwise obscure pathway. He declares, "I am the way and the truth and the life" (John 14:6). The Way stood before them. They knew the Way all the time! But they didn't know they knew.

The main subject of Jesus' declaration is the way to the Father. He finishes the verse above "No one comes to the Father except through me." The concepts of truth and life only expand and expound the way.

1. They tell us that Jesus is the *true* Way. In the third "I Am" saying Jesus declared himself as the Good Shepherd (and the Door) of the Sheepfold. He says, "All who ever came before me were thieves and robbers" (John 10:8).

A Muslim woman, speaking through a Parsi interpreter to a group in Gujerat, India, said that the sun rises in the east and shines into every window of the house. Every window represents a different religion, and each window thinks it has the light. Jesus was a window and Buddha was a window. But the sun shone through them all.

Her Parsi interpreter disagreed, saying, "I beg to differ from the lady. Jesus is not just a window. He is the sun shining into these other windows."[4]

Peter—made bold by the Holy Spirit—proclaimed to the rulers and elders of the people, "Salvation is found in no one else, for there is no other name under heaven given to men by which we must be saved" (Acts 4:12). Jesus claims exclusive right as the Way to the Father.

2. Jesus is also the *living* way. The writer to the Hebrews declares, "We have confidence to enter the Most Holy Place by the blood of Jesus, by a new and living way opened for us through the curtain, that is, his body" (10:19-20). A supreme paradox is that Jesus opens a *living* way by *dying.* He died to live. Christ calls His disciples to a symbolic, but certain, death to sin.

Once upon a time there was a beautiful garden. The master of the garden expressed great pride in his plants. But he reserved a special place near his heart for the beloved bamboo tree.

One day the master came to the bamboo and said, "Bamboo, I would use you." The bamboo was overjoyed. In his master's words all his hopes, aspirations, and dreams became flesh.

Drawing himself to his full height, he replied, "Master, I am ready. Use me."

"Bamboo," the master continued, "in order to use you, I must cut you down."

"Cut me down? Use me, Master, but please don't cut me down."

"Bamboo," explained the master, "unless I cut you down, I cannot use you."

"Master, if you cannot use me unless you cut me down, then do it."

"Bamboo," the master continued, "in order to use you, I must also strip your leaves and branches from you."

"Please, no!" Bamboo exclaimed. "Cut me down, but please don't deprive me of my adornment."

"I can't use you unless I do," he replied.

"Then do it."

"Bamboo, if I would use you, I must also divide you in half and cut out your heart." Very submissive now, Bamboo only nodded his head.

So the master cut down Bamboo, stripped his branches and leaves, and cut out his heart. Then he took him to a very dry place in his field where a spring of cold, sparkling water bubbled up out of the ground. He laid one end of Bamboo into the pool and the other end into the water channel in his field. Soon, water gurgled along the Bamboo into the thirsty field.

The days came and went, the rice was planted and grew, and finally the harvest came. Only then did once glorious Bamboo realize that his master could only use him *when he was broken*. But then he became a channel of life to his master's world.

If we are ever to be channels of blessing to our spiritually thirsty world, we, too, must be willing to be broken, to die with Christ to sin.

Evil men broke the body and life of God's Son on a cross. But in His brokenness He put back together a world shattered by sin. He laid down His life as the Way to heaven.

Heaven. Who will take us there? We shall walk home to heaven by the Way—and the Truth and the Life—Jesus.

6

I am the true vine.

JOHN 15:1

On Your Mark! Get Set! Grow!

When Jesus uttered His final "I Am" saying, the fruit of the vine was still sweet on the lips of His disciples (Mark 14:25). Jesus often used feasts or signs as occasions to present spiritual truth, and He did it again here.

In one of His most vivid metaphors, Jesus described the intimate relationship between himself and His disciples. He called himself the Vine and His disciples the branches of the Vine.

A.   The Faithful Vine

To the Palestinians in Jesus' day, the vine was a familiar figure. So common was it that the Maccabaean coins carried its inscription to represent Israel. The Psalmist writes:

> Thou hast brought a vine out of Egypt: thou hast cast out the heathen, and planted it. Thou preparedst

room before it, and didst cause it to take deep root, and it filled the land. The hills were covered with the shadow of it, and the boughs thereof were like the goodly cedars. She sent out her boughs unto the sea, and her branches unto the river (Ps. 80:8-11, KJV).

"It is a curious fact," says William Barclay, "that the symbol of the vine is never used in the Old Testament apart from the idea of degeneration."[1]

God, speaking through Jeremiah and addressing himself to Israel, questions why, after He "had planted thee a noble vine, wholly a right seed: how then art thou turned into the degenerate plant of a strange vine unto me?" (Jer. 2:21, KJV). Hosea derides Israel as "an empty vine, [who] bringeth forth fruit unto himself" (Hos. 10:1, KJV).

Israel, the intended vine, failed to yield acceptable fruit in the eyes of the Gardener. Against the background, Jesus appears as the faithful, productive Vine. Under the careful eyes of the Gardener, He will yield favorable fruit.

The branches inhere in the vine and receive their life from it. There are two kinds of branches: the fruitless branch and the fruitful branch.

B. The Fruitless Branch

Jesus says, "If anyone does not remain in me, he is like a branch that is thrown away and withers" (John 15:6).

1. The first step in the process of fruitlessness is *separation.* One summer my wife, Jan, and I planted some flowers. After we had deposited each in its assigned space, one displaced petunia remained. I decided to plant it in an unadorned corner near the front door of the church.

One day the doorbell rang, and a small neighbor friend held up the lone petunia. "Will you give this to Jan?" he asked. He had only wanted to share some of earth's beauty with a friend, but he had unknowingly separated the plant from its life source, the earth. Had I not replanted it, it would certainly have died. If we become separated from the vine, we, too, will die spiritually.

2. The second step in the process of fruitlessness is *withering*. When the branches become separated from the vine, they produce no fruit. They begin to wither and die.

At certain times of the year the Law required the people to bring offerings of wood to kindle the sacrificial fires in the Temple. They could *not*, however, bring the wood of the vine. It was too soft for any useful purpose. Only the fruit of the vine is useful; the unproductive branches are worthless, and the keeper of the vineyard must destroy them. They "are picked up, thrown into the fire and burned" (ibid).

3. The third and final step in the process of fruitlessness is *separation*. Christ allows no room in His vineyard for unproductive branches. Separation from the vine brings a final and irrevocable separation from Christ at the end of life.

God's judgment, however, also affects a person while he lives. Someone has said that in this universe something terrible happens when a man separates himself from Christ.

Judas epitomizes the unproductive branch. When Satan sowed the seed of rebellion in Judas' fertile heart, something awful took place. John—who paints spiritual word pictures in two major colors, black and white—says of Judas, "As soon as Judas had taken the bread, he went out. And it was night" (John 13:30).

The night in his soul obscured the light, the truth, his moral sanity. When the betrayer had finished his terrible task, "he went away and hanged himself" (Matt. 27:5).

Let us never allow the process of fruitlessness to suck us down into its awful maelstrom. How can we avoid fruitlessness? By consciously choosing to remain firmly engrafted into the living Vine.

C.   The Fruitful Branch

The fruitful branch abides in the Vine. Jesus promises, "If a man remains in me and I in him, he will bear much fruit" (John 15:5). What does it mean to abide? In everyday living, abiding translates into obedience. A. W. Tozer writes:

> The church of our day has soft-pedaled the doctrine of obedience, either neglecting it altogether or mentioning it only apologetically. . . . The Bible knows nothing of salvation apart from obedience. . . .
> To obey, in New Testament usage, means to give earnest attention to the Word, to submit to its authority, and to carry out its instructions.[2]

In his walk with Christ, the disciple encounters two specific crises of obedience. At the risk of oversimplifying the majestic grace of God in the human heart, I mention these crises briefly.

In the first crisis of *conversion*, the unconverted person confesses and repents of committed sins and receives forgiveness. In the second crisis of *entire sanctification*, the Christian makes an entire commitment of his life to God and is sanctified wholly.

But the road of obedience does not end there. Following conversion, the Christian has continued in obedience up to the second crisis. At this point he does not sink in the stagnant pool of spiritual passivity. Rather, he gains access onto the superhighway of holiness (Isa. 35:8). The Spirit frees him to grow much easier and much faster. Abiding in Christ involves both crisis and continual obedience.

1. *No Christian can bear fruit apart from union with the Vine.* Jesus declares, "No branch can bear fruit by itself; it

must remain in the vine. Neither can you bear fruit unless you remain in me" (John 15:4).

In His discourse on the Holy Spirit, Jesus alluded to the principle of abiding: "Because I [the vine] live, you [the branch] also will live" (14:19). And if we remain engrafted into Him, the opposite is also true—"I can do everything through him who gives me strength" (Phil. 4:13).

2. *The abiding branch bears fruit.* Jesus teaches a lesson, not about other branches, but about the spiritual qualities of Christian character. He refers not to soul winning but to character building.

It is interesting that Paul, when speaking of the Christian's produce, uses the word "fruit" instead of the word "work." A man can work apart from a source; but a spiritual branch *cannot* bear fruit apart from the life-giving Vine.

Jesus includes the first two out of three of the first cluster of fruit Paul records in Gal. 5:22-23—*love* and *joy.* Most commentators, however, agree that love is a bowl which holds all the other fruit of the Spirit-filled life.

The Master reminds us that wholehearted obedience produces deep joy. He says, "I have told you this so that my joy may be in you and that your joy may be complete" (John 15:11).

The world grasps greedily for a few moments of pleasure. And they are usually not disappointed. Most everyone can squeeze a few fleeting moments of pleasure out of their lives.

But abiding, deep joy eludes them. Satan tantalizes them, hangs a semblance of joy out before them as if suspended on a string, and jerks it mockingly. But it is all just beyond their reach.

To complete the trinity of the first cluster of fruit, the Bible adds *peace.* The abiding Christian reaps a rich harvest of peace, as Paul wrote: "The peace of God, which transcends all understanding, will guard your hearts and your minds in Christ Jesus" (Phil. 4:7). Like soldiers guard a captured city or defend an outpost, God stands guard over our spiritual lives.

Let us also remember that God does not dump this fruit into our laps full-grown so that we have them ever after. If He did, they would spoil! They are dynamic. They grow. They cannot be stored for future use.

Also, we need not despair because we have no finished products to display. Every Spirit-filled Christian ought to possess *all* the fruit of the Spirit. But each may not possess them in the same degree. Each fruit produces more and more under the watchful care of the Gardener.

3. *The fruit-bearing branch submits to pruning.* "Every branch that does bear fruit he trims clean so that it will be even more fruitful" (John 15:2). In order to produce, the vine requires much attention. In Palestine the keeper of the vineyard prunes the young vine and does not allow it to produce for the first three years of its life. But when pruned, the vine produces so profusely that the slips are set out 12 feet apart to allow for its abundant production.

Donald Metz says that the vine-branches metaphor illustrates a second work of divine grace in the soul. The converted Christian bears fruit. The sanctified Christian—after pruning—bears *much* fruit.[3]

The pruning symbolizes the cleansing work of the Holy Spirit. When Jesus tells the disciples, "You are already clean because of the word I have spoken to you" (John 15:3), He means they are potentially clean. Later Jesus would pray for the Father to sanctify them (17:17). The *potential* cleansing became *actual* on the Day of Pentecost (Acts 15:8-9).

W. E. Sangster tells how London disposes of its waste. Large ships carry the sludge—that waste which cannot be salvaged for some useful purpose—down the Thames to

Black Deep, a depression in the ocean floor 15 miles off Foulness.

There the vessels open their valves, and in 20 minutes, the sludge sinks down through the salt, aseptic sea into Black Deep. For a few minutes an ugly wake surrounds the ship. But the ocean is so great, the sea so briny, and the hole so deep that within an hour water samples reveal not even a hint of the foulness of the sludge. The sea has swallowed it up and cleansed it in the process.

John Wesley knew a deeper abyss than Black Deep. He knew a cleanser more powerful than the salty sea—the love of God. He translated the third verse of a German hymn like this:

> *O love, Thou bottomless abyss,*
> *My sins are swallowed up in Thee!*
> *Covered in my unrighteousness,*
> *Nor spot of guilt remains on me*
> *While Jesus' blood through earth and skies,*
> *Mercy, free, boundless mercy! cries.*[4]

While we remain in Him, He keeps us clean and makes us spiritually productive.

Reference Notes

Chapter 1:
1. The chapter title is from Luke 15:17, NIV.
2. Dan Morgan, "The Roots of Hunger," *Natural History*, October, 1977, p. 118.
3. Claire Sterling, "Death Stalks the Thirsty Sahel," *Reader's Digest*, June, 1974,. p. 80.
4. William Barclay, *The Daily Study Bible*, "John," vol. 1, rev. ed. (Philadelphia: The Westminster Press, © 1975), p. 215.
5. W. Glyn Evans, ed., *He Has Come* (Nashville: Broadman Press, 1975), pp. 54-55.
6. W. T. Purkiser, Richard S. Taylor, and Willard H. Taylor, *God, Man, & Salvation* (Kansas City: Beacon Hill Press of Kansas City, 1977), pp. 318-19.
7. Evans, *He Has Come*, p. 83.
8. Lee Fisher, *Out of This World* (Plainfield, N.J.: Logos International, 1970), quoted in *Decision*, October, 1970.

Chapter 2:
1. Kenneth L. Wilson, *All Things Considered* (Chappagua, N.Y.: Christian Herald Books, 1977), p. 22.

Chapter 3:
1. There are really seven "I Am" sayings. But since "I am the Door" and "I am the Good Shepherd" are so similar, I have treated them together and called them the third "I Am" saying.
2. William Barclay, *John*, Daily Study Bible series (Philadelphia: Westminster Press, 1956), 2:65.
3. E. Stanley Jones, *Abundant Living* (Nashville: Abingdon, 1942), p. 32.
4. Phillip Keller, *A Shepherd Looks at Psalm 23* (Grand Rapids: Zondervan, 1970), pp. 33-34.
5. *Ibid.*, p. 37.
6. Purkiser, Taylor, and Taylor, *God, Man, & Salvation*, p. 34.
7. Keller, *A Shepherd Looks at Psalm 23*, pp. 104-5.
8. Barclay, *John*, 2:69.
9. *Ibid.*, 2:78.
10. Helen Smith Shoemaker, *I Stand by the Door* (Waco, Tex.: Word Books, 1978), pp. 9-11. The chapter title is taken from this book.

Chapter 4:

1. Grace Nies Fletcher, *Preacher's Kids*, Reader's Digest Condensed Books, vol. 4, 1958 (Pleasantville, N.Y.: The Reader's Digest Association, Inc., 1958), pp. 38-40.

2. E. Stanley Jones, *Abundant Living* (Nashville: Abingdon, 1942), p. 12.

3. Nevil Shute, *A Town like Alice*, Reader's Digest Condensed Books, vol. 1, 1976 (Pleasantville, N.Y.: The Reader's Digest Association, Inc., 1975), pp. 478-80, 496-97.

Chapter 5:

1. William Barclay, *John*, Daily Study Bible series (Philadelphia: Westminster Press, 1956), 2:180-81.

2. W. E. McCumber, "Manipulating Second Advent Doctrine," *Herald of Holiness*, April 1, 1978, p. 18.

3. E. Stanley Jones, *The Divine Yes* (Nashville: Abingdon, 1975), p. 147.

4. Edward Hastings, ed., *The Speaker's Bible*, vol. 11: *The Gospel According to St. John* (reprint ed., Grand Rapids: Baker Book House, 1971), p. 72.

Chapter 6:

1. William Barclay, *John*, Daily Study Bible series (Philadelphia: Westminster Press, 1956), 2:201.

2. A. W. Tozer, *Paths to Power* (Harrisburg, Pa.: Christian Publications, n.d.), pp. 14-15.

3. Donald Metz, *Studies in Biblical Holiness* (Kansas City: Beacon Hill Press of Kansas City, 1971), p. 123.

4. W. E. Sangster, "How to Begin Clean," *Decision*, May, 1962, p. 3.